Villains

poems by

JeFF Stumpo

Finishing Line Press
Georgetown, Kentucky

Villains

Copyright © 2016 by JeFF Stumpo
ISBN 978-1-944251-39-0 First Edition
All rights reserved under International and Pan-American Copyright Conventions.
No part of this book may be reproduced in any manner whatsoever without written permission from the publisher, except in the case of brief quotations embodied in critical articles and reviews.

ACKNOWLEDGMENTS

Some of the poems in this collection first appeared in the following publications:

Villanelle in royal blue: *Coldfront*
Villanelle with unrequited narcissism, Villanelle dyed white, purple, and green: *The Laurel Review*
Villanelle mistaking womb for wound: *Delikanli*
Villanelle that fell for the wrong man again, Villanelle in Babel: Drunk in a *Midnight Choir*

Additionally, *Coldfront* published a lyric essay on the writing process of blending an old form with new tricks. You can find it in their Poets off Poetry section at www.coldfrontmag.com.

Editor: Christen Kincaid

Cover Art: JeFF Stumpo

Author Photo: JeFF Stumpo

Cover Design: Elizabeth Maines

Printed in the USA on acid-free paper.
Order online: www.finishinglinepress.com
    also available on amazon.com

Author inquiries and mail orders:
Finishing Line Press
P. O. Box 1626
Georgetown, Kentucky 40324
U. S. A.

Table of Contents

Villanelle in royal blue 1
Villanelle with unrequited narcissis 2
Villanelle that fell for the wrong man again 3
Villanelle mistaking womb for wound 4
Villanelle questioning a pop culture phenomenon 5
Villanelle dyed white, purple, and green 6
Villanelle to all you sucka MCs 7
Villanelle in an unfairly-stereotypical small town 8
Villanelle cornered in a stall in the boys' bathroom 9
Villanelle with Polish boy bending a fence with his mind 10
Villanelle with radioactive crackle 11
Villanelle that is not now nor ever has been 12
Villanelle seen many more times than it will admit on record . 13
Villanelle with dead man chosen for the rhyme 14
Villanelle enlisting the ACLU 15
Villanelle calling, "Pretty bird. Pretty bird." 16
Villanelle thinking it's Sherrie Levine but coming out
    Richard Prince 17
Villanelle ghosting Gethsemane 18
Villanelle in Babel 19
Villanelle with slow decay 20
Notes 21

Villanelle in royal blue

After all, the bottle said, "Drink me,"
and I've a complicated relationship with authority.
And I've always loved to read

a book with a hard swallow of whiskey
in the morning, holding the glass philosophically.
After all the bottle said, "drink me"

was the thing that concerned me least.
"Bring the gun." "Is it so hard to steal?"
and "I've always loved to read

a woman's fortune in her legs as she sneaks
out of her house, married
after all." The bottle said, "Drink." Me,

I was never in any shape to disagree,
not the author of my own mor(t)ality,
and I've always loved to read

a hard life's lesson in a good book. Leave
it in the book, because my way is easy.
After all, the bottle said "Drink me,"
and I've always loved to read.

Villanelle with unrequited narcissism

Could miss you but I don't, so,
baby, sweet baby, sweet little baby,
let the lights go

out over LA, New York, Boston, Chicago.
Let those other men know they maybe
could miss you, but I don't, so

keep on calling. I'm not at home.
You thought you'd make this a carnival fantasy,
let the lights go

rolling on like a merry-go-round, oh,
rolling on like a Ferris wheel.
Could miss you but I don't so

much miss you as know the itch of you, though
you weren't no dog in heat. Baby, please
let the lights go.

Let that hope down slow.
I'm rolling on like a stone, see?
Could miss you but I don't, so
let the lights go.

Villanelle that fell for the wrong man again

She scrubs the dishes
and through her skin.
Wishes on wishes

are a handsome man's kisses,
her mother told her, still thin.
She scrubs the dishes

and thinks on more fishes
in the sea, her mother again.
Wishes on wishes

in stacks so precious
are still worthless as a bad man's grin.
She scrubs the dishes,

scrubs, sobs, hitches,
scrubs where his hand had been
wishes on wishes.

Ramblin' men may be delicious,
but you can't keep them in the end.
She scrubs the dishes,
wishes on wishes.

Villanelle mistaking womb for wound

Who would have thought that pregnancy would be
announcing itself like this?
Considered a disability,

Charmaine's thoughts often raced due to ADHD,
but in this instant because the doctor said this:
"Who would have thought? That pregnancy would be

unplanned, yes? Well, here's some literature to read.
How do you plan to tell your boss this?"
Considered a disability

by most of the long-time employees,
Mr. U_____ could barely come to terms with this.
"Who would have thought that pregnancy would be

popping up just when we're most in need?
I don't know that I can give you time off for this."
Considered a disability,

Charmaine read, by ADA decree.
That was her way out of this.
Who would have thought that pregnancy would be
considered a disability?

Villanelle questioning a pop culture phenomenon

What's in your head? Zombie
outbreaks, zombie infestations,
zombie, zombie

everything, and why? Feel
surrounded by evil manifestations?
What's in your head? Zombie

viruses, zombies on TV,
zombies in suits, zombie fascination
zombie. Zombie

as TV, as drug, as refugee,
as asked during confrontation:
"What's in your head?" Zombie

after brains; who gets away free?
Zombie Troubles and zombie Haitians,
zombie, zombie

Katrina, zombie wiki,
Zombie Foxconn automation.
What's in your head, zombie,
zombie, zombie?

Villanelle dyed white, purple, and green

I am the pied piper piping his pipe
to an odd tune. You have heard
I am you were you free? To be freed by the night,

you embraced the bat, to be a cat with a rat, slight
variations on reincarnations, still part of the herd.
I am the pied piper piping his pipe

to an odd tune you have heard. Ripe
for the picking, this city, so shitty. My word.
I am you were you free. To be freed by the night

takes more than a mask; you must change your face, white
where was black and vice versa.
I am the pied piper piping his pipe,

and Gotham's children of all ages abide.
I change even the rhymes you have heard.
I am you. Were you free to be freed by the night

you would join me, not fight.
All cards would be wild, all worlds our world.
I am the pied piper piping his pipe.
I am you were you free to be freed by the night.

Villanelle to all you sucka MCs

This is my track
meet. You trippin' on cracks in the street.
You just backin' that

fat beat. I'm 175 of man
and muscle. You empty cuz you hustle. Please,
this is my track

record: I don't lack records. I make black
records like Glasper makes radio, G.
You just back in that

saddle, addled, same horse, same stream. I got a knack
for innovation, always addin' to my team.
This is my track,

my trade, just call me Jack.
You fade. You lose. You got a two-bit dream.
You just backin' that

bad play, MC. This is my track,
my way, home free.
This is my track—
you just backin' that.

Villanelle in an unfairly-stereotypical small town

Now they can't say he didn't give it his all—
broke the all-time record for touchdowns by two,
and the best of him's recorded on the Athletics wall,

and his signature's on the State Game winning ball.
His mama says it's a game for a fool.
Now, they can't say he didn't give it his all,

was first in his class, another placard, if small.
Got his girlfriend pregnant on the first time, too.
The chest of him pinned her to the motel room wall,

and she squealed his name and to God she called,
and called on both again when the stick turned blue.
Now they can't say he didn't give it his all

when he drank his last beer at the VA hall,
and if he was underage, well, what can you do?
The heft of him leaned on the VA wall,

and he was halfway between a lurch and a crawl,
and nobody says they saw the .22.
Now they can't say he didn't give it his all,
when the rest of him's wasted on the motel room wall.

Villanelle cornered in a stall in the boys' bathroom

He says he'll leave the way he came
in a minute, staring you down.
If you give up your name

as a first-grader, you can't be the same
kid again. You have to hate something somehow.
He says he'll leave the way he came,

and you wonder how often he plays this game.
No. You don't. You just freeze and cower.
If you give up your name,

you give up whatever future you might have claimed,
trade it in dreams only for a cowl.
He says he'll leave the way he came,

and you know that you can't go that way,
can't go home to home because now,
if you give up your name,

no bathroom is safe.
But he's waiting here with a grin and a growl.
He says he'll leave the way he came
if you give up your name.

Villanelle with Polish boy bending a fence with his mind

Whose hands are these
in leaden fists? Who are you
to separate the strong from the weak,

you evil alchemists, murderers, Nazis?
Why are my nights made of glass and blown through?
Whose hands are these

that reach out and touch no one, seize,
and cannot break the falls of dead Jews?
To separate the strong from the weak

you put on cat masks, played hide and seek
with mice destined to lose.
Whose hands are these

that reach out and touch no one, seize
only air, and yet seem to feel every barb, every screw?
To separate the strong from the weak

requires inhuman will and inhuman means.
And suddenly I know what I must do.
Whose hands are these
to separate the strong from the weak?

Villanelle with radioactive crackle

If it were my call?
Can't count how many guys that day
I knew. Amal

or Amir or Amon or Jamal
or whatever, I didn't know their names.
If it were my call

they'd fly just up to their virgins then fall
straight into hell's flames.
I knew 'em. All

of 'em have…had…have…families, shawled
wives and crying kids. And all you can say…
If it were my call…

I'll admit it, I bawled
when I heard about the towers, the planes.
I knew 'em all.

All it takes now is the balls
to stand up and say,
if it were my call,
I'd nuke 'em all.

Villanelle that is not now nor ever has been

Gold for bombs. Bombs for slaughter.
Few older tales are told.
Mr. Midas meets his daughter

on the steps of the factory, has bought her
a dolly. But is he coming home tonight? No.
Gold for bombs, bombs for slaughter

are Mr. Midas's trade. He got the ear
of a senator during a war that ran cold.
Mr. Midas meets his daughter,

now grown, near the Capitol, sought here
by men who know anything can be sold.
"Gold for bombs. Bombs for slaughter,"

she leans in to chastise her father
but draws silent seeing suits approach.
Mr. Midas metes his daughter

out to those who will deny they've caught her,
but Reds like her are worth their weight in gold.
Gold. For bombs, bombs for slaughter,
Mr. Midas metes his daughter.

Villanelle seen many more times than it will admit on record

"Is this war just?" The politician, Puntz,
adjusts his tie, speaks clearly,
"I think I've seen this in a movie once,

how the reporters think that just because
they're the Press they can speak with impunity.
Is this war chest the politicians'," Puntz

pauses, "or the media's?" Ungrateful runts,
he thinks them. He repeats,
"I think I've seen this in a movie once,

how nobody remembers whose fault it was
or whether there was even fault to see.
Is this war just the politician, Puntz,

or is it every one of you as well? Grunts
are dying, yes, overseas.
I think I've seen this in a movie once,

and at the end, an injured soldier still stands in front
of his flag, a servant of his country."
Is this war just? The politician punts.
I think I've seen this in a movie once.

Villanelle with dead man chosen for the rhyme

Gun rhymes with one,
as in Oswald or Booth,
but also a million

other assassins
with which history is shot through.
Gun rhymes with won,

as in Final Solution,
not just what Nazis or Cambodians do,
but also a million

other nations
(like the Red, White, and Blue?).
Gun rhymes with one,

as in the institution
intimidating Oulu
but also a million

other daughters and sons.
So which are you?
Gun rhymes with one
but also a million.

Villanelle enlisting the ACLU

I am a medusa mirror look, the voice from the burning book, all
that the old gods know, even the one whose [   ] was severed,
redacted for parents staring slack-jawed, shock and awed

that such violence could permeate and still build the pyramids, y'all.
I'm an ox-head on a fish hook, a map—X marks de Sade, lover—
a medusa mirror look, the voice from the burning book, all

that the old rappers know plus flow plus a big pair of brass [Walt
banned in Boston. *Knock a Star* challenged in Austin.] Shove it up your
[redacted for parents standing slack-jawed, shock and awed]

Let me break that down for you like my man, Octavio Paz:
[I pledge allegiance to the flag of the United States of America
and to the Republic for which it stands, one nation, under God]

Damn. Y'all must have been reading that in Arizona. Caw! Caw!
I'm a shrapnel kestrel covered in petrol. Light me on fire and wish me
    luck, mother-
[redacted for the parents staring slack-jawed, shock and awed]

Don't you love your nation blue-eyed and blonde
and straight and playing baseball and party-line voter?
I am a medusa mirror look, the voice from the burning book, all
redacted for the parents standing slack-jawed, shock and awed.

Villanelle calling, "Pretty bird. Pretty bird."

We are judge and jury of the Age
of Industry. We glut on iron and gore.
Your sentence, "A caged

bird that sings is never done for." Page
after page, such hopeless hope bursts forth.
We are judge and jury of the Age

of Information. Your sons in jail rage
or in tenements drain. We say IQ. We say inborn,
your sin, tense, a cage

constructed out of devolution. Sages
we must be. Take our tests. Look at our scores.
We are judge and jury of the Age

of Ages, measured with our gauges,
the best of all possible worlds. Do not scorn
your sentence, "A caged

bird sings." Why else build this stage?
Please, sing for us some more.
We are judge and jury of the Age.
Your sentence: a cage.

Villanelle thinking it's Sherrie Levine but coming out Richard Prince
after Terrance Hayes

We sliced the watermelon into smiles.
We sliced the watermelon into smiles.
We sliced the watermelon into smiles.

We sliced the watermelon into smiles.
We sliced the watermelon into smiles.
We sliced the watermelon into smiles.

We sliced the watermelon into smiles.
We sliced the watermelon into smiles.
We sliced the watermelon into smiles.

We sliced the watermelon into smiles.
We sliced the watermelon into smiles.
We sliced the watermelon into smiles.

We sliced the watermelon into smiles.
We sliced the watermelon into smiles.
We sliced the watermelon into smiles.

We sliced the watermelon into smiles.
We sliced the watermelon into smiles.
We sliced the watermelon into smiles.
We sliced the watermelon into smiles.

Villanelle ghosting Gethsemane
after Borges

This is the Word.
Jesus was a man (un)like you or me.
I was trying to save the world,

and Scripture said he was a Pearl
of great price, but his life that had to be.
This is the Word.

It was fate, not hate, no pieces of silver
on a silver plate. That is one way to see.
I was trying to save the world.

Or perhaps in the end I was closer
to the master than the others, one of true belief.
This is the Word,

that I was the only one who knew he would return.
Now comes version three, so listen most carefully.
I was trying to save the world,

so I took the seven sins and twisted and curled
them into a noose and hung sin incarnate from a tree.
This is the Word.
I was trying to save the world.

Villanelle in Babel

The song the singer's singing's about sin.
It's Pride and Lust and Greed and Lust again.
And I'm no believer, but I don't believe I can win.

A voice above a voice that tries to rise above the din
remarks on penises or, then again, on pens.
The song the singer's singing's about sin

that's bearing us or burying us in gold up to our chins,
these golden chains, unholy chains, we fettered men.
And I'm no believer, but I don't believe I can win.

This is the music, what can we do but listen in,
be swept along and swept away by waves when
the song the singer's singing's about sin,

shortcutting past our brains, our conscious caves in,
unlike reading, whether *Alette*, the lays, or *Gravesend*.
I'm no believer, no longer believe that I can win.

A chord hits quick and precise as a pin.
My mind and heart and knees are made to bend.
The song the singer's singing's about sin,
and I'm no believer, but I don't believe I can win.

Villanelle with slow decay

And one day you wake up and like the taste of coffee.
One day you wake up, and the price is raised on tolls.
And one day you wish you had learned to dance for real.

One day the caffeine asks, "For whom does the bell peal?"
One day someone calls your humor "droll."
And one day you wake and fire up Mr. Coffee.

One day your bands are sellouts instead of indie.
One day nobody remembers your favorite rock 'n roll.
And one day you wish you had learned to dance for real.

One day you're less Blu-ray and more reel-to-reel.
One day you're more whiskey and less Sol.
One day you wake up and drain last night's coffee.

One day they've grown tracts over your favorite trees.
One day you're too tired to put the flag out on the pole.
And one day you wish you had learned to dance for real.

One day you roll over, and there is no she.
One day even your thinning bones are cold.
And one day you wake up and hold nothing but your coffee.
And one day you wish you had learned to dance for real.

Notes

Each poem in this collection was written to a soundtrack, a song or two put on repeat for anywhere from thirty to sixty minutes. While most of these pieces do not directly derive from their song's lyrics, and while the collection stands perfectly well on its own, I feel that there is another layer to the experience to be had if one listens to the "soundtracks" while reading the pertinent poem several times.

In the order in which they appear in the manuscript:

Villanelle in royal blue:
    Howlin' Wolf—"Moanin' at Midnight"
Villanelle with unrequited narcissism:
    Howlin' Wolf—"Smokestack Lightning"
Villanelle that fell for the wrong man again:
    Cat Power—"Ramblin' (Wo)man" & "Metal Heart"
Villanelle mistaking womb for wound:
    Megan Spellman—"In this corner..."
Villanelle questioning a pop culture phenomenon:
    The Cranberries—"Zombie"
Villanelle dyed white, purple, and green:
    Morphine—"Super Sex (Live@the WMBR-FM, MIT Campus, Cambridge, MA '93)" & "Radar (same)"
Villanelle to all you sucka MCs:
    The Robert Glasper Experiment—"Black Radio"
Villanelle in an unfairly-stereotypical small town:
    Neko Case—"Prison Girls"
Villanelle cornered in a stall in the boys' bathroom:
    Nirvana—"Polly"
Villanelle with Polish boy bending a fence with his mind:
    Metallica—"Nothing Else Matters"
Villanelle with radioactive crackle:
    Metric—"On a Slow Night"

Villanelle that is not now nor ever has been:
   XXXXXXXXXXXXXXX
Villanelle seen many more times than it will admit on record:
   State Radio—"Calling All Crows"
Villanelle with dead man chosen for the rhyme:
   Billie Holiday—"Strange Fruit"
Villanelle enlisting the ACLU:
   J. Kingz (Aesop Rock vs Portishead)—"NY Electric / Cowboys"
Villanelle calling, "Pretty bird. Pretty bird.":
   Thrice—"Come All You Weary"
Villanelle thinking it's Sherrie Levine but coming out Richard Prince:
   Phillip Glass & Wendy Sutter—*Songs & Poems for Solo Cello*
Villanelle ghosting Gethsemane:
   Saul Williams—"Tr(n)igger"
Villanelle in Babel:
   Mumford & Sons—"Broken Crown"
Villanelle with slow decay:
   Neko Case—"Red Tide" & "Marais La Nuit"

Jeff Stumpo has been a bookstore owner and a part-time professor, a slam poet and an apologetic telemarketer. He is the author of four professionally-published chapbooks, including this one, and an album of spoken word. His wife is the smart one. His daughter is four going on fourteen. His dogs are nuts. He has a website at www.jeffstumpo.com.

www.ingramcontent.com/pod-product-compliance
Lightning Source LLC
Chambersburg PA
CBHW060227050426
42446CB00013B/3213